Robert E. Lee

BRAVE LEADER

Robert E. Lee

BRAVE LEADER

by Rae Bains
illustrated by Dick Smolinski

Troll Associates

Library of Congress Cataloging in Publication Data

Bains, Rae.
    Robert E. Lee, brave leader.

        Summary: Traces the life of the highly respected
Confederate general, with an emphasis on his difficult
boyhood in Virginia.
        1. Lee, Robert E. (Robert Edward), 1807-1870—Juvenile
literature.   2. Generals—United States—Biography—
Juvenile literature.   3. United States. Army—Biography—
Juvenile literature.   [1. Lee, Robert E. (Robert Edward),
1807-1870.   2. Generals] I. Smolinski, Dick, ill.
II. Title.
E467.1.L4B25   1986   973.7'3'0924 [B] [92]   85-1092
ISBN 0-8167-0545-3 (lib. bdg.)
ISBN 0-8167-0546-1 (pbk.)

M 3764

Robert E. Lee

BRAVE LEADER

Day after day, week after week, eight-year-old Robert Lee waited for letters from his father. They were almost the only things that made Mama smile. Robert noticed that little else made her smile these days. There were money problems, and she wasn't feeling well. Most of all, Mama and everyone else in the family missed Papa. Even four-year-old Catherine, who could hardly remember him, missed her father.

Henry Lee had gone away to live in the West Indies. Mama said he might never be able to return to Virginia again. He had to leave because he owed a large number of debts, and was unable to pay them. If Mr. Lee had stayed home, the authorities would have thrown him into debtor's prison. In the early nineteenth century, that was the punishment for people who couldn't pay their debts.

Henry Lee had been in debtor's prison twice before. Each time, his family had to sell some property to pay his debts and have him released. This time, however, there was not enough money and not enough property left to sell.

Robert was just a child, but he understood why his father was away. The boy often thought of that day in June 1813 when his father left. Robert was only six years old then. But he could not forget the sight of his mother weeping as she waved a final farewell. Nor could he erase the picture of his father, standing at the rail of the ship as it sailed for the island of Barbados.

Life was confusing to young Robert Lee. Everyone knew that Papa had done some foolish and bad things. But Mama spoke of Mr. Lee only as a great hero of the American Revolution. Robert's brothers, Carter and Smith, told him that Papa had been Virginia's best governor. These things were true. If only Robert could forget the bad times . . . .

Robert Edward Lee was born on January 19, 1807, in a lovely mansion called Stratford. It sat on a grand plantation in Westmoreland County, Virginia. The house was huge and furnished with the finest things money could buy. But often the doors had to be kept shut with chains. That was the only way the Lees could keep out the bill collectors. While Robert enjoyed living in the wonderful mansion, he could feel the gloom and sadness that haunted his parents.

When Robert was three years old, the Lee family moved to the town of Alexandria, Virginia. They had been asked to leave Stratford. The mansion belonged to another son of Mr. Lee's from a previous marriage.

Stratford had originally been owned by Mr. Lee's first wife. She left it to their son, Henry Lee, Jr., when she died. The first Mrs. Lee did

not want to leave Stratford to her husband
because she knew how foolish he was about
money and property.

When Henry Lee, Jr. reached the age of
twenty-one, he inherited Stratford. Until that
time, his father took care of the estate for him—
but he had not taken care of it very well. Now
Henry Lee, Jr. wanted Stratford for himself.

There was another reason for the move to
Alexandria. Charles Carter Lee, called Carter,

was almost twelve years old. Ann Lee was ten years old. Sidney Smith Lee, called Smith, was eight years old. Mrs. Lee felt they should be in proper schools, with other children their own ages. Alexandria had good schools, and the Lees had many relatives there. It seemed a perfect place to settle.

Even after Mr. Lee left the country for good, the family stayed in Alexandria. It was a pleasant town, right across the Potomac River from the city of Washington, D.C. The town of Alexandria wasn't large, but it had everything a child like Robert could want. There were docks along the river, where ships came from ports all around the world.

The young boy liked to sit and watch the bales of tobacco and cotton being loaded onto the ships. Workers unloaded cloth, machinery, furniture, and all kinds of foreign-made goods. Robert also liked to listen to the sailors talking in different languages, and to see their unusual clothing.

There was much to do in Alexandria. On warm days, Robert went swimming in a little cove, just outside the town. He also ice-skated there on cold winter days.

As much as he liked Alexandria, Robert liked another place even more. He loved the estate called Shirley, situated on the James River. It was a huge property, spread over twenty-five thousand acres of land. It had forests, land-scaped lawns, streams and ponds, and large sections used for farming.

The plantations of Shirley produced corn, wheat, vegetables, cotton, and flax. Workers harvested fruit from the plantation's orchards. Its streams and ponds were an endless source of fish, and its forests yielded deer, turkey, and other wild game.

There were long rows of chicken houses, pens
filled with geese and ducks, and herds of cattle,

18

dairy cows, horses, pigs, goats, and sheep. Except for sugar, spices, coffee, machinery, and some clothing, everything the occupants of Shirley needed was produced on the sprawling plantation.

Shirley belonged to the Carter family. Mrs. Lee, who was a member of that family, was always welcome there once Mr. Lee was out of the country. She and her children enjoyed these visits very much. Robert especially looked forward to playing with his many cousins who either lived there or—like him—were visitors.

Robert also spent many hours watching the blacksmith shoeing horses, the millers grinding grain into flour, the carpenters repairing and making furniture, and the many other crafts-people at work. There were also hundreds of slaves on the Virginia plantation. Some worked as house servants, some as mechanics, and some as farm laborers. With all the people at Shirley— family, friends, visitors, and workers—the plantation was as busy as a small city.

Robert's mother had twenty-two brothers and sisters, each of whom had children. In fact, there were so many children in the family that the Carters ran two schools to educate all of them. The girls attended one family school at Shirley. The boys attended the other family school at Eastern View. Eastern View was the plantation in Fauquier County, owned by Elizabeth Carter Randolph, one of Mrs. Lee's sisters.

Until Robert entered the boys' school, at the age of nine, he had not attended any other school. But he did know how to read, write, and do arithmetic. When he was little, Robert's mother was his teacher. After a while, her place was taken by the tutors who lived at Shirley. This kind of education was normal for the children of wealthy families in the South at that time. Virginia had no public schools then. Private schools existed, but they were not for young children.

Robert, his brothers, sisters, and cousins were expected to be well-educated by the time they were adults. However, there was no planned system of education. It was simply understood that they would acquire an education for the same reasons that they would learn to dance, to ride a horse, and to behave properly in company.

Robert took easily to the life at Shirley, where his family spent more and more time. He was a quiet, thoughtful, and very bright boy. Whatever he set out to learn, Robert learned thoroughly. He soon became a fine horseman, marksman, and athlete. He was quite polite, and showed a knack for doing the right thing in adult company.

Robert was so serious and proper, in fact, that some of his cousins teased him about it. He never got into trouble, and adults often held him up as an example to the other children. Still, Robert was liked by his cousins. They knew family problems caused him to be so serious.

Robert had a difficult childhood in a number of ways. There was his father's disgrace, which he heard adults discuss quite often. Mrs. Lee's money problems troubled him, too. Being at Shirley was wonderful, but it was like taking charity. The horses he rode weren't his, nor was the food he ate, the bed he slept in, or the servants who waited on him.

Robert saw himself as a poor relation who had to earn his keep by being a perfect gentleman. He had to prove that the Lees were respectable, worthy people. It was as if, by his exemplary behavior, Robert hoped to blot out his father's bad reputation.

Robert attended Eastern View for close to two years. In that time, he proved to be a fine student. He also was able to relax a bit at Eastern View. His aunt, Mrs. Randolph, was an easygoing person who encouraged the boys to laugh and have fun. Robert would always look back on his years at Eastern View as one of the happiest periods of his childhood.

In 1818, tragedy struck the family, and Robert returned to Alexandria. His father, after years of exile, had finally sailed for home. But he died on the voyage from the West Indies. His death crushed Mrs. Lee, who had never stopped hoping that their family would be reunited.

Even though he was just eleven years old, Robert knew he had to be the man of the house. His brothers and older sister were away. Carter was finishing his law studies at Harvard University, and Smith was about to begin a career in the United States Navy. Robert's sister, Ann, was in Philadelphia, receiving treatment for tuberculosis. Only his younger sister, Catherine, who was just seven, was at home.

Robert did not hesitate to take over adult responsibilities. He did the marketing, managed all the housekeeping, directed the servants, paid the bills, looked after the horses, and saw to everything else that needed to be done. Being the man in their Alexandria home was the way Robert tried to make life easier for his mother. But taking care of the house was only one of his concerns. He also accompanied Mrs. Lee on daily carriage rides, read to her, told her jokes, and made sure she took her medicine every day.

The youngster was extremely well organized. With all his duties, he also found time for fun. Robert and one of his cousins, Cassius Lee, loved to hunt ducks and catch fish, and did so often. They also practiced boxing and fencing,

which were sports popular with Virginia gentlemen of the time.

The street fairs that came to Alexandria were
special delights for the boys. They saw puppet
shows, booths with magicians, fortunetellers,
and games of chance. Robert and Cassius never
missed a fair when one came to town.

29

One of Robert's favorite activities was going to the horse markets. From the time he was very young, Robert E. Lee was a horse lover. Everything about horses interested him, and he was considered a fine judge of horses. Robert learned about horses by watching the sales at the market, by asking questions of the dealers, and through personal experience gained by riding and caring for horses. His relations didn't hesitate to ask the youngster's advice before buying an animal for racing or for pulling a carriage.

Years later, when Robert E. Lee was a military officer, his experience at the horse market proved extremely valuable. His horsemanship won him the respect and admiration of both officers and troops. Furthermore, Lee insisted that his army acquire the best horses. He couldn't be fooled on the price or quality of the animals.

Perhaps the most important lesson Robert learned at the horse market was how to communicate with all kinds of people. While the grooms, traders, and blacksmiths at the market were not educated gentlemen, they were wise in the ways of their world. Young Robert learned from them, and came to respect them. In turn, they responded to his friendship.

Lee's ability to get along with everyone served him well when he commanded Confederate troops in the Civil War. More than any other general of his time, Robert E. Lee inspired a loyalty and love from his soldiers. His soldiers had enormous respect for him, but they never feared him. Any soldier could approach the general with a problem or a complaint.

When Robert was twelve, his mother enrolled him at the Alexandria Academy, on Washington Street. The schoolmaster, Mr. William B. Leary, stressed Latin, Greek, and mathematics. Mr. Leary was glad to have Robert as a student. The boy did well in all his subjects, especially in mathematics.

Robert attended the Alexandria Academy for three years. During that time a special bond developed between him and Mr. Leary. In many ways the schoolmaster became a substitute for the father Robert did not have.

When Robert finished his studies at the academy, he faced a major decision: which career should he follow? He could not afford to live as a gentleman without a good job, and his mother could not afford to send him to college. This meant he would have to learn a trade or enter military service.

The idea of serving in the United States Army appealed to Robert. It was a chance for him to follow the path his father had taken. "Light-

Horse" Harry Lee was still honored for his glorious deeds during the American Revolution. The fame of Harry Lee was still as bright as ever in military circles.

Robert also hoped to make a name for himself —a great name. In some way, he wanted to make Virginians forget the shame his father brought to the Lees in his later years. More than anything, Robert wanted to be well respected in Virginia. He considered himself a devoted Virginian with a deep loyalty to the state.

Late in 1823, sixteen-year-old Robert told his family he wanted to go into Army service. They all approved wholeheartedly. In fact, at a gathering of the Lee clan, someone suggested that Robert ask for an appointment to the U.S. Military Academy at West Point, New York. There, he could get a free college education and train to be an officer.

With the excellent military reputation of his father and letters of recommendation from a number of important Virginians, Robert E. Lee was accepted by West Point in 1824. But, he was told, he would have to wait a year. There were so many applicants ahead of him that Robert could not be admitted until July 1, 1825.

Until that time arrived, Robert continued his studies at a school near the Lee home. It was run by a schoolmaster named Benjamin Hallowell. Years later, Mr. Hallowell wrote, "Robert E. Lee entered my school in the winter of 1824–1825 to study mathematics, preparatory to his going to West Point. He was a most exemplary student in every respect. He was never behind time at his studies, never failed in a single recitation, was perfectly observant of the rules and regulations of the institution. He imparted a neatness and finish to everything he undertook. The same traits he exhibited at my school he carried with him to West Point."

Robert E. Lee entered my school
in the winter of 1824-1825
to study mathematics,

Robert E. Lee entered West Point at the age of eighteen. His four years there set standards that are still regarded with awe. Lee earned the distinction of never receiving a single demerit in four years. How good was that?

In those days, the superintendent of the Academy kept a book with a page set aside for each cadet. On this page, all the demerits were entered as a permanent record. Lee's conduct was flawless, and his page did not have a mark on it. In fact, by his third year, his page was given to another cadet who was always in trouble. In addition to his perfect behavior, Lee was graduated second in his class academically.

After he was graduated in 1829, Second Lieutenant Robert E. Lee rushed home to Alexandria, where his mother was gravely ill. She died soon after his return. Robert took the death very hard. His only consolation was that his success at West Point had made his mother happy.

In the seventeen years between Lee's graduation and the beginning of the Civil War, he served at various Army posts. He was a captain in the Corps of Engineers in the Mexican War. He was superintendent of West Point from 1852 to 1855. After that tour of duty, Colonel Lee commanded the Department of Texas. This was before Texas became part of the Union.

Lee was nearing retirement when the nation was split apart in 1861 by the Civil War. That year, he was offered a high command in the fight against the South. Though he was a Southerner, Colonel Lee prepared to accept the offer. Before he could say yes, however, Virginia seceded from the Union to join the Confederacy.

Robert E. Lee had always felt a deep sense of loyalty to Virginia. When his state seceded, he promptly resigned his commission in the U.S. Army. The deciding factor in his choice of service was the defense of his native state.

THE
UNION
IS
DISSOLVED!
VIRGINIA SECEDES

As a Confederate general, Robert E. Lee was a brilliant and well-loved commander. But not even his valiant leadership could change the war's outcome. The North had more troops and supplies, and it was only a matter of time before the South would be defeated. That time came on April 9, 1865, at the town of Appomattox Court House, Virginia. On that day, Robert E. Lee, commander-in-chief of all Confederate armies, signed the surrender and gave his sword to General Ulysses S. Grant, leader of the U.S. Army.

Intending to spend his remaining years quietly, Lee retired to his Virginia home. But he was immediately offered the presidency of Washington College (now called called Washington and Lee University), in Lexington, Virginia. He accepted and served in that capacity until his death on October 12, 1870. His passing was mourned in the North as much as the South, for the nation had lost a great man.

Date Due			

m 3764